notes
from my
inner child

notes
from my
inner child:
i'm always here

Tanha Luvaas

NATARAJ
PUBLISHING

© 1992 Tanha Luvaas

Published by Nataraj Publishing
P.O. Box 2627
Mill Valley, CA 94942

Cover design: Kathy Warinner
Illustrations: Kathy Warinner
Text design & typography: **T·H** Typecast, Inc.

Library of Congress Cataloging-in-Publication Data

Luvaas, Tanha, 1946-
    Notes from my inner child : I'm always here / by Tanha
Luvaas
        p. cm.
    ISBN 1-882591-10-0 (acid-free paper) : $8.95
    1. Inner child. 2. Luvaas, Tanha, 1946- . I. Title.
BF698.35.I55L88 1992
155.2'5—dc20   93-14955
                                        CIP

First Printing, March 1993

ISBN 1-882591-10-0

Printed in the United States on acid-free paper

10   9   8   7   6   5   4   3   2   1

contents

contents

Part 3: My Story 47

My Search for Myself

My Life in My Room

Getting to Know Her

Psychology of the Selves

Building Our Relationship

Writing with the Opposite Hand

What it Was Like Being with My Child as We Wrote

What Happened Inside Me During the Writing

How Different Aspects of My Child Emerged

Problems with Listening Intensely to Just One Voice

Getting the Male and the Female Together

Meditation

to the lost
children
inside everyone

acknowledgments

To Shakti Gawain for believing in me and seeing me all these years, way before I knew I had any worth or knowing.

To Jon, my partner, for all the love and support that came through in helping me learn the male things needed to bring this book into form and for making it through those horrid times when I messed up the computer.

To Susan, who knows in ways that are beyond words and whose very presence always reminds me.

And to all the people who've been my teachers and supporters through the years.

foreword
by shakti gawain

Until a few years ago, I didn't know I had an inner child. Like most rational, worldly adults, I assumed that childhood was something I had appropriately left behind many years ago. In fact, I had scarcely been a child at all, since I was serious and responsible at a very young age.

So imagine my surprise when, in my own healing process, I began to experience within me the very real energy of a sensitive, vulnerable young child. Strange as it seemed, the little girl I once was still lived inside of me, with all the same feelings, needs, and spontaneous natural wisdom that I had so effectively buried long ago. At first I felt rather embarrassed and awkward about her existence. Gradually, I have learned to love and value her, and to integrate her energies harmoniously into my adult life.

Tanha Luvaas has been an important part of that process. One of my dearest friends, she is probably more deeply in touch with her inner child than anyone else I know. She has profoundly helped and supported me in opening to and caring for my child.

Getting in touch with one's inner child is a vital step for anyone committed to a deep level of emotional healing. The child holds the key to our feelings, creativity, sense of fun, and ability to enjoy real intimacy. Listening to the inner child is a doorway to our spiritual essence, as Tanha so beautifully shows us in this book.

Her book has touched me deeply. I hope it will help you know and love your own special inner child.

With love,
Shakti Gawain

introduction

Once when I was having a therapy session, my facilitator asked if she could be with my inner child. She said I could move anywhere in the room where I felt my child would like to be so that she could talk with it. I had seen and talked to my inner child once before in a guided visualization, but that was different from letting my inner child speak to someone else. So, although I was quite skeptical that my child would really be there just by my moving into another place in the room, I decided to go along with my facilitator's suggestion as an experiment.

As soon as I moved into a different spot in the room, which was just for my child, I started crying and crying and crying. There were no words. There was just a rich feeling of warmth and relief that flooded my body. I remember thinking, "This seems really weird, but it feels so good—like I'm at home. I wish I could feel this way all the time."

My facilitator said, "This is your inner child you're experiencing. Let's just let her be here so you can really get the feeling of what it's like to have her energy filling your body." For the next five or ten minutes we were both silent, and I allowed myself to fully experience the deep richness of her presence. My body felt as if it were submerged in water, and there was a feeling of warmth and closeness with myself. There was a lack of anxiety, an emotional wholeness, a connection with myself that made me feel safe and close and cuddly.

That experience changed my life. Without even knowing it, I had always felt like a lost waif inside, but acted like a perfectly together woman outside. Connecting with the part of me that felt like a lost waif and feeling, as a result, a deep connection with her made me want to explore this inner child business as fully as possible. It has been an eight-year exploration, which led to this book. This "waif" has turned out to be a dear friend I have grown to cherish. Whenever I feel her fear, her anger, or her need, I've learned to acknowledge and attend to that feeling.

I can't always give her what she wants, but being able to feel and hear her calling to me by experiencing the sensation of discomfort in my body has shown me that when she feels my attention on her she can relax.

Often, as she feels my willingness to accept her as she is and speak up for her when necessary, the pain seems to subside and a deeper, more spiritual part seems to arise. It feels in the moment as if my natural beauty and wisdom are able to emerge and her woundedness is no longer there.

We are made up of many parts or subpersonalities. They each have a value and a function and a way of operating that is distinctly different from the other parts. The inner child is just one of them, although it was the earliest to form and is, perhaps, the most *essential*.

In the process of exploration and experimentation with my inner child, I have used four wonderful tools that have helped me to see, feel, and hear from her: visualization, voice dialogue, journaling with my nondominant hand, and meditation. I'll explain more about each of these methods later. Because my child, the other parts, and I have built a relationship of such trust and respect, I now feel an inner support and strength I never felt before.

The first part of this book consists of words that came directly from my inner child, written through my left, non-dominant hand. She seemed to express herself differently each day. Sometimes I recognized her as the "waif," other times as the more essential natural being that isn't wounded. Some days, she would start as the waif and end as the natural being. I never knew what to expect.

The second part of this book is a dialogue with my child and with some other opposite parts of me who needed to speak in order for my life to be in balance. I wrote questions with my dominant hand, and the opposite parts responded with my nondominant hand.

The last part of this book contains my story of our journey together, with more about the tools I've used to get in touch with her. I tell you about my life before she came and my life since, and what we've learned together. I share some mistakes I've made by getting so carried away with her energy that I didn't give as much value to the opposite energies inside of me.

Some people writing about the inner child say that we are on a journey of healing our inner child. My experience is that my child doesn't need healing. What needs healing is my connection with her; my trust and belief in her wisdom, guidance, and direction for me. Many of us have hidden our child, and there are other parts, too, whom we have hidden and really need in order to express the balance of our power and vulnerability.

Whether we know it or not, we are all on a road to recovery, trying to reclaim the selves we have hidden. We are also learning to salvage what's real in us from what we have been told we are supposed to be. It's a big job, after having been taught all our lives to repress most of our true expressions. I have found my inner child to be immensely helpful in this process of recovering my more essential, personal self.

One of my concerns in writing this book is that you understand that it's a description of my own unique process with my inner child. It's about my journey with my child and the other parts that arose as we spent each afternoon together. That doesn't mean my child is like yours or that if you're with your child the same thing will happen for you. This isn't a book about the "way it is."

I'm especially concerned that you understand this point because I came from a very rigid religious belief system that made it impossible for me to have any faith or trust in my own understanding of God or of reality. This belief system was one of the most harmful experiences of my childhood because I learned to doubt my own instincts, feelings, and perceptions and accept someone else's. My hope is that whatever I write will not be used as dogma by my readers. I believe that part of our uniqueness as human beings comes from how we perceive and structure our reality according to our own conceptual framework.

I have had many wonderful teachers in my life. I have absorbed what they had to offer and adapted it to my own unique understanding and experience. I hope you can do the same with this material—not trusting me as an authority, but trusting you.

part 1:

from my inner child

i live inside of you

There are three reasons why I want this book written. I want everyone to know that I live inside them and they can trust me. And I want you to know, Tanha, that I'm really here and if you'll be my friend and listen to me, then things will be much easier and more fun and better in your life. And I want the world to know me and value me, because there are loads of people who throw me out and then never want me back. And without me there is no real, deep satisfaction in life and nothing works quite right.

No kidding. I live way inside you and I always have ever since you were a kid. I've never left and I'm still here. I want to play with you. I want you to find me again and ask for me, and if you do I'll come to you and show you my existence. I'll tell you what I need from you and give you the guidance you long for and the closeness you have always been trying to find outside.

I'm waiting for you to admit that something is hurting or something is missing. When you're sad and lonely or empty or needy or bored or dissatisfied, don't run from those feelings, for there I am way deep under all this pain, way deep down inside under all that you feel. I have a message for you and you'll sense what it is if you'll just be willing to be with the sensations in your chest or heart or gut.

I have so much to offer you and to offer the world if everyone in the world could start reconnecting with me again. Even underneath the anger there I am, waiting for you to connect with me. It's too hard being a grown-up without any connection to me. It's not fun and it's not intimate. It feels as if something is missing and it feels dry and without love or joy.

You had to put aside all my most tender, vulnerable feelings and pretend I wasn't there. You had to do that to survive in your family. When you wanted to have some control and

8

power and success in the world, you had to leave me behind
because the world is afraid of how vulnerable I feel and
there hasn't been much place for me there. I've remained
hidden, locked away in some deep-behind-the-stairs-closet
that you didn't even know was there. I want you to find me.
I want you to start listening to me and stop abandoning me.

WHY YOU HAD TO ABANDON ME

This is why you had to abandon me and hide me. I was a
baby. I could do nothing for myself. I needed so much love
and attention that if I got the message from the outside, "You
shouldn't do that," I stopped doing it. I stopped doing whatever I was doing if there was disapproval for it, and I started
doing the things there was love and approval for.

Instead of doing what I felt like doing and what felt
good to me, I started doing what was wanted from the outside. I needed approval. I don't know if you understand
when I say I *needed* it. I mean without it I would have died.
So you and I started separating and becoming two.

We did what we had to do to survive. You started hiding
me and becoming whatever your parents and family and
teachers and friends and society and religion wanted you to
be. You had to, because if you hadn't, our love supply from
outside would have been cut off. And we all know that babies
need warmth and love and attention and food to survive. In
other words, you buried me—hid me, shut me up, repressed
me, suppressed me, denied me, betrayed me, abandoned
me, and all-around ignored me. It was necessary for you to
do that when you were growing up, but it's not necessary

anymore. I'm very much alive and well and waiting for you to reconnect with me.

Here's more about how the separation between you and me happened. You were taught to focus on what was happening outside you rather than on the natural sense of what was needed, which I give you from inside. You were taught to listen to what your parents and teachers needed from you rather than to trust and listen to what I might be telling you. You were taught that everything you needed was outside you. You were never taught to listen inside for my guidance or to trust me.

You see, if your parents had thought of me as a being of magnificent light connected with the knowingness of the universe, who took on a body to enter this earth plane, they would have had great respect for me and my choices and desires and they would have mostly supported me in the directions I chose. I don't know much about living in the down-to-earth practical way; they could have taught me how to do all that and learned from me about all the rest. But, they weren't taught to trust themselves, either, so they couldn't trust me. They wanted to do their best and be good parents. So they did what their parents did to them or they did the opposite of what their parents did, but they were almost always trying to do their best. And they usually succeeded in making a good little robot out of you who did what they did and what society wanted.

It brought about a terrible split inside us when you had to listen and then act on all the outside influences instead of listening to me. It seems as if everyone who is living in civilization has to deal with the disease that this split creates when they are taught not to trust themselves. This lack of trust in my goodness is the sickness of our society and our world. This split between you and me is what makes you always feel dissatisfied and wanting more. What you're really wanting is the reconnection with me, and you're trying to find me by getting more success and money and status and friends and lovers and sex and eating and drinking and drugs and TV and movies and entertainment.

I'm not in those things. I'm inside whatever is happening in your body the moment you stop to feel me. If you're frustrated, there I am under the feeling. Experience the sensation in your body and you've got me back. Don't just think about the feeling, but feel where it is in your body and there I'll be, waiting for you. After you acknowledge what is being felt, whether it's an emotion or an emptiness or uncomfortableness, then I can start emerging. Sometimes I have a message for you.

I'm waiting for you to reconnect with me again so I can start giving you my gifts—all the treasures I have for you. For I am all your feelings and your natural wisdom. I am vulnerability and magic. When you start listening to what I say and need and reveal to you and you start responding to me, you start living in a brand new way because I can show you how to have heaven on earth.

GET TO KNOW ME

It's really the time for people to learn to connect with me, because without me everything gets into a big mess. All people need to know me inside them and learn how to be a good parent to me, the kind they always wished they could have had. That way all the conflicts and hurts and wounds people have with each other have a chance of being healed.

Without knowing me, there really can't be open-heartedness and gentleness, compassion and understanding. Without me there can be only power plays and power struggles; that's what happens between people who don't know how to show each other the child in them. And that's what's happening on a big scale among our countries. So what I'm saying is that it's even a matter of survival on this planet for people to get to know me, and be able to care for me, and give me what I need, and be able to communicate my feelings and needs and desires to each other.

I'm one of many valuable parts that make you who you are. But I'm the part of your personality that's closest to your essence. I'm your link to feeling and then beyond that to spirit. I live in your body. You sense and perceive me there.

Do what it takes to find me again. You won't be sorry.

WHAT I'M GOOD FOR

I can take you out of your head, out of the way you think things should be into the way they really are. I live in your body and respond to what's happening now. I can tell you whether I like what's going on or whether I hate it. I can tell you whether it feels good to be where you are or whether you should leave. I can tell you where you need to be, to feel good, and who you feel good with. Your head gives you many messages about whether you should like someone or not, but I tell you whether you *do*. Your head tells you what you should be doing to make people like you or to get or keep a job, but I tell you what you *really* want to do.

I'm the part of you that responds to life in the moment. Your thoughts live in the past and the future, but I live in the body and respond to whatever is going on around you. I am the child—my function is to yell when I'm hurt, cry when I need something, get mad when I'm ignored. I have certain needs for security and closeness, warmth and sleep, respect and attention.

I can tell you why you're feeling strange things in your body. Remember how every time you thought about your good friend Sally you felt kind of a sick feeling in your gut? You asked me and I told you what it was. And then you checked it out with her and she *had* been judging and blaming us behind our back. I can give you messages you aren't conscious of through what you sense in your body. You can check them out with reality. But I was worried that I would tell you I thought she was judging us and you'd check it out with her and she wouldn't be aware she was judging us and then you would believe her and not me.

Your not noticing or believing what I'm trying to say is such a painful thing. I'm still afraid you'll believe everyone else more than you believe me because that's what you were taught to do when you were a kid and that's what you've been doing all your life, until you started getting close to me again.

I'm really glad you're beginning to trust me. I may not always be right; we'll just have to keep finding out together whether I am. I guess I'm as thrilled as you when I find out that I am.

WHAT HAPPENS WHEN YOU DON'T HEAR ME

When I feel you're not listening to my needs, I start screaming and complaining, and crying louder and harder. I start making your life difficult until you hear me. If things start going wrong in your body, that's me trying to get a message to you. If things go wrong in your work and your relationships, stop long enough to listen and hear me.

I am trying to be heard. If you have a car wreck or a heart attack, know that I am here screaming some message into the night and you're not hearing—you who are too busy taking care of others to hear me, you who are too busy trying to prove to others how great and what a success you are, you who are too busy going after money, you who are simply like a little wind-up toy or robot trying to fulfill some parent's or spouse's or church's or society's expectations, without ever hearing me or knowing what I want or have to give.

This is what makes me feel angry and irritated, depressed and dissatisfied, scared and lonely, hopeless and helpless—this feeling of not being heard.

Your doctors and psychiatrists are so funny. They look at a person's disease or illness and all they can think about is how to cut it out or get rid of it. They still don't get that it's just me trying to tell you something that I need or want or something that happened that felt terrible. The grown-up robot won't let me have or talk about my very real feelings, and here they are all bunched up inside in a bundle of disease and illness. It's just me, dying inside from lack of attention and caring. It's terrible being locked away in here all these years, with the person I live in never feeling or knowing my value. It's so incredibly frustrating.

I'm like a magnificent racehorse being kept in one stall of a dark barn. And each day I'm fed grass when what I really need and crave and want is oats, but the owner doesn't trust that I know what I want so she listens to her more practical part and feeds me grass. She doesn't really have time to play with me or ride me because she's so terribly busy being an important person. So day after day I am kept in this dark stall in this dark barn not being used. I am a Kentucky Derby winner at heart if she would just listen to what I need to eat and let me show her my stuff. I am a magnificent winning horse with incredibly beautiful energy, and I am rotting from lack of being used, seen, and valued, or acknowledged, known, and recognized.

WHAT HAPPENS WHEN YOU DO START LISTENING TO ME

When you do start listening to my loneliness or fear, my longing or anger, my despair or worthlessness, my hopes and dreams, you start giving me the love and attention I've always needed. First I start to feel, wow, I really do exist and my feelings really are valid. Then I don't feel so terribly alone and cut off. From there we can start being a team, we can start building a relationship. You can start believing in me, that what I'm good at doing, feeling, and sensing is good for us, is the motivator for a wonderful way of life that really is our birthright.

If you listen to me and act on what I want sometimes, or just hear what I'm saying, instead of only listening to your head, you may very well get in trouble with the outer people in your world, but inside you would feel a lot better because you were being and acting the same as I feel. Then you'd feel this warm feeling of being connected with me—that you're not alone because we're finally together working as a true team. When you feel how good it feels to finally be with me, you'll start to feel an inner core of support, a sense of sturdiness that feels so strong and good inside that it'll be okay even if some outer people stop liking us.

Every time you let me express the way I feel in your body's language or your face's expressions or your body's action or your words, then you'll feel that warm closeness of you and me being really connected and you'll feel empowered.

Many other parts of you may be frightened of your being so real. They are the parts that have been in charge. One may be the part that has always told people what they wanted to hear rather than what I felt, so that people wouldn't be offended and stop loving us. You may also hear a practical, survival part of you that says you can't really do what I say because it may put us at risk financially. And you may hear a very critical part of you that makes you feel really wrong for letting me exist and have my voice.

All your life you've been given lots of reasons why you shouldn't listen to me or trust me, so this change from not listening to me to trusting and respecting and believing in me is not one you're probably going to make overnight. You'll probably have to build a relationship with me and really get to know me before you can begin to realize how much I can bring you. Probably it will take years for all the cells of your body to trust our connection. Maybe all your life. Everything good takes time.

You wouldn't believe the things that happen in your life the closer you get to me. When you're listening to me, you'll get your fondest heart's desire if you express what I really need and reach for it. As you trust me more and more and let me lead and guide you, that is when the magic starts.

ONE OF MY FONDEST DESIRES

You see, one of the fondest desires of my heart is to be known by all people for who I really am. I am their soul in the form of their inner child and from the beginning I could have been acknowledged and respected and allowed to lead them, but they seem to have strange ideas that I came to earth in a state of sin and need redeeming. What really needs redeeming is that point of view, for it leads parents to instruct their children and not to get the benefit of their children's instruction and not to get the benefit of their children's wisdom; it doesn't allow the parents to see the world through my eyes of awe and wonder. The truth is that I'm the closest thing to God on this earth other than nature and animals. If you let me, I will keep showing you why I came to earth. You'll see my purpose emerge by seeing what I love to do. You'll begin to understand what I'm naturally good at and how I naturally act. You'll see what I came to learn and came to contribute. You'll see me, rather than the little robot clone you want me to become. You'll allow me to set my own pace, and you'll be there to really support what I'm doing. And you'll teach me how to physically survive on earth.

part 2:

dialogues

dialogue between tanha
and the inner child

T*anha:* How do you feel about being hidden within people?

I've needed to be hidden. You don't understand; I've needed it. I am so precious—like a precious gem. I think of the quote: "Don't throw pearls before swine." People wouldn't treat me well because they don't value or believe in my true worth. They only think of controlling and civilizing me. I had to be hidden.

Tanha: Most people in the western civilized world would say you had to be taught how to live in the world—that without controlling you and making you obey them and share what you have with them you'd be a selfish, wild little curse. What do you say about that?

If I am crossing another's boundary and violating that person, I must be told so that I know. If what I am doing bothers people, I must be told they are bothered. That is the only education I need about being with people. That is how I learn. I don't need to be shamed or controlled. That is done only because people don't know who I am. They are totally blind to my natural wisdom, and they don't know I exist inside them.

Tanha: How could someone treat you as you want and deserve to be treated?

Love me as I am. Learn from me and see the way I do things. Answer my questions as simply as possible. Be happy. Trust me that I really know what I love, what I came here for, and support me in doing it. Understand me and respect me when I show you and tell you about my feelings and thoughts and desires. Know that who I am and what I choose is right and is enough for me. You can tell me you don't like my choices, but only as a way of sharing who you are, not as a way of controlling me.

Tanha: How do you communicate with people?

There are lots of ways I try to tell you things. When your body feels uncomfortable, it's almost always me! I'm trying to let you know something's wrong and I need your attention. Because people don't know I'm here trying to be heard and they don't know how to listen to me, it's really terrible. They don't get my important messages, so I have to scream louder and louder to get their attention. Usually that's when their bodies get sick. It's me screaming, and when that doesn't work and I really have an important message, I'll do things that really stop them so they'll have a better chance of listening—like car wrecks or broken bones or heart attacks or cancers. That's usually after I've been screaming for so long that I've given up. It's too late to hear me because I've given up.

Tanha: I keep feeling your pain in my body. There's such a loneliness I find when I feel that pain. What do you need?

I need you to want to be with me above all else. I need you to stop leaving me. I need you to shine your love and light on me. I need to be the center of attention. I need your love and attention.

Tanha: Is there any special way for me to give you that?

You can love me as I am and trust that my needs are important and worthy of your respect, support, and daily time and attention. I want you to spend time with me.

Tanha: Tell me more about how I can hear you.

Close your eyes and ask for me. Notice what you feel and where you feel it in your body. Ask the feeling or sensation you're experiencing what it wants to say. Stay with the sensation and soon you'll get a sense of what it may be needing to express. You may hear its words or just get a sense of it. You may not trust what you're hearing at first. That's not unusual. It's usually just the skeptical voice in us that doesn't want us to believe any of these silly things because we may be disappointed if no one is there or we may feel really foolish. It takes a little time to learn to do this.

Tanha: One day when I sat down to write, my throat felt really tight as if I was being choked. I took a moment to sense the uncomfortable feeling in my body, then I asked it, "What would you like to say?" I sensed that its reply was, "Don't leave me out. I am here, too, and I count, too, but I don't know who I am." So I said, "Tell me something about you. Who are you?"

25

A line on a white arrow.
A voice never spoken.
A time never come.
I write poems I don't know the name of and songs that
    have never been sung.
I care about being heard, and those times I stood up in
    the corner at family talk night I would have loved to
    speak, but nothing I
could say would have been right or good enough.
I'm judged and condemned before I ever reach
    consciousness.
I am the silent voice with so much to say.
I am so precious and so unaccepted.
What I might say wouldn't fit the bill.
I might cry or I might be silly and say stupid things that
    don't fit or look pretty. I wouldn't do it right.
It's not possible for me to do it right; someone else does
    that!
I just create.

When people ask for me, I love telling them what I think
and feel about things and I love giving my input and advice
and I love being listened to. You see, everyone has shoved
me aside and discounted me for so long that I'm full of wisdom
I really want to share. Do you know how awful it is to be
discounted and considered worthless for thousands of years?
    I am your inner child, inner wisdom, inner strength, inner
creativity, inner mother, inner feminine, inner nurturer, inner
playfulness. I have many sides to me, all of which seem to be
simple, timeless, loving.

I am an experience, not a thought or an idea. You can sense me by experiencing the uncomfortable sensations you may feel from time to time in your chest, solar plexus, or other places in your torso. If you stay with the uncomfortable feeling, soon you'll get a sense or a feeling of what I want to say.

Or when you feel tightness or tension in your torso area, you can write to me with your dominant hand and ask, "What's the matter?" Then with your focus of attention on the uncomfortable feeling, put the pen in your nondominant hand and I'll answer.

Ask me what I love, what turns me on. Go ahead and try it. Get some blank paper and with the hand you usually write with, ask me what I really like. And with the hand you don't usually write with, let me answer.

Tanha: What do you really like?

I really like things that make me feel good, like warm baths when I'm cold and cold baths and swimming when I'm warm. I like friends who like to hear from me and really listen to me and see me. I like feeling loved and cared about. I like it when you or anyone else is really interested in me. I like you to spend time with me and hear whatever I want to say, and feel whatever I'm feeling and love me as I am.

Tanha: If people saw you for who you really are, how would they treat you differently?

They would allow me to set my own pace, and they would be there to really support what I am doing.

Tanha: What are you feeling so sad about today?

I just hate it when you leave me. I am you and without me life is so small, dry, and unreal. It's not worth leaving me to impress anyone. When you leave me, that's the real pain. Stay with me to do your thinking. I am your feeling sense in your body. A new kind of thinking comes through, that arises out of the body and the moment and not out of habit, when you stay with me to do your thinking.

When people try to act a certain way rather than express how I feel inside them, they become helpless and vulnerable because they aren't connected to my real sense of things inside. That connection has been cut. They are left with this "trying-to-act-as-they-think-they-should," according to what others may want. This feels like a shell that is walking around doing the right things without the living creature inside it. And the living creature is left out there in the world with no shell around it. What a vulnerable feeling.

Now can you understand why you have felt so incredibly vulnerable all your life? The healing we are doing by your learning to trust me and believe in me is what's putting the shell back together with the living creature inside it. Just keep listening and trusting and believing, and know we'll be one.

You have believed for so long that I was this inadequate, not-enough, wounded, needy, vulnerable, terrified child. That's not who I am. I feel very open and small, but I don't feel helpless if you acknowledge my need or speak up for me. The only reason I have felt so alone and terrified and abandoned and afraid to face the world and get all the things I want is because I haven't felt your support. I haven't felt you were there to really notice me or speak up for what

I feel and want, and what I like and don't like, and what
I need and don't need.

Yesterday when the bank lady said we would have to
pay $25 in service charges for the overdrafts and you really
felt my grief and you heard me say it's not fair, you were
willing to support my feelings. That's what makes me feel
safe enough to go out in the world, because I know you're
supporting me and believing in me. When she said no and
you called her supervisor to stand up for my feelings, it felt
so good. It means you believe I'm worth something. I have
felt worthless because you haven't believed in my worth.
When you do, I feel more powerful, more valuable, and
I have more to give us.

When you became aware of your spiritual nature from
your meditation retreats, remember how little and unimpor-
tant you made me feel each time? You found your soul and
all that limitless expanse of our being and you wanted to
dump me. Gosh, we have had some hard times. It's only
now because you are writing this book that you're willing
to spend some consistent time with me, hearing what I have
to say.

Tanha: Are you angry with me?

I guess I do feel some anger at your lack of loyalty to me.
You've been willing to be so supportive and available to
everyone you call a friend; but you know what? You haven't
been nearly so good to me. All these outer friends get all
your attention. When you're with people, don't you know
that if you listened to me you would feel the magnificence of
my energy? I would be able to flow through you to other
people, and you would flow out my love and you wouldn't

have to try so hard to please them. Because when we're together it just feels good; and other people would feel how good we feel together and would love us for being ourselves instead of trying to be interesting or smart or strong.

Tanha: As we write this dialogue each day I'm developing a respect for who you are and feeling the empowering effects of learning to support your feelings and desires by communicating them to others. I'm beginning to feel I'm not alone—as if we're a team and you're this wonderful bright child living right inside me.

I'm seeing you as something more real than feelings, someone who lives here inside me and has great confidence that if I'm there for you, we'll work things out together. The more confidence and self-esteem you feel from me supporting you, the more powerful I feel.

You have influenced my life in such a positive way. How do you want to influence other people, my dear inner child?

I want people to discover that I live inside them.

Tanha: What do you believe that will do for them?

They'll start to experience more richness, satisfaction, and intimacy in their lives. And they won't feel alone. They'll feel supported the more they know me. They'll feel compassion for all who live and breathe.

Tanha: Is there a name I should call you?

I have a changing face and name. Sometimes I am the Knowingness of the deep inner feminine whose source is Divine Universal energy, and other times I am simple as a child. I am mother and child, wisdom and love and compassion.

I cannot be contained. I must be given out to the hungry and thirsty world, for it has been so long without me. If I had to give you a name for myself, it would be Soul-Woman-Child. I have no form, you see, and yet I have this deep sense of knowing and wisdom.

Tanha: Tell me about how we became separated.

At first we were one. Then, mommy wanted us to smile and daddy wanted us to be quiet. It was then that we became separated. I continued being and knowing, while you put your attention on doing whatever made mommy and daddy happy. You responded to your outside world, and gave them whatever they needed. You couldn't tolerate their not being pleased with us. It was most important to you to make sure they were happy. You did anything and everything to make them happy. You knew what they needed, and you jumped to make certain they were taken care of. That became your sole responsibility and purpose in life. It was as if we were plugged into each other in the beginning and you took that plug out and put it into mom and dad.

This is why you've needed and wanted to spend so much time alone, because in these alone times you've felt safe enough to disconnect the plug from the outer world and put it into me again. And you've felt so relieved, as if you've finally come home. When you have reconnected with me you have felt deep tears of joy and relief, for I am your heart and soul. Without me you are like the tin woodman and the cowardly lion and the straw man.

Things have been so crazy and empty and painful for people who have pulled their plugs from me. They are really like empty shells with no life in them. The animal has left and the poor shell keeps trying to fill its empty feeling with work and money and lovers and sex and food and drugs and alcohol and shopping. . . .

I am still here throbbing and pulsing with aliveness. You can find me by becoming aware of uncomfortable sensations in your body or by simply asking for me.

Tanha: How are you hurt by me?

I am hurt by you when you do not hear me, see me, feel me, and believe in me. I'm a real person. I am part of you and I have a strong sense of how things need to happen or need to be in order for something to occur. I am here to guide you and help you to be where you need to be, and I'm here to give birth to what is most needed.

The reason you have felt so lost and vulnerable and needy and afraid is that you lost your connection to me. Without my guidance, you are lost and helpless and fearful and terribly needy. You are like a very young child who has lost her parents and doesn't know who she is or where she is.

My mission is to let the world know that I exist inside of everyone. There is far too much pain without me, and it's time you took an easier route—with *me*!

Even while you're reading this book you may notice how differently you feel as you let me affect you. What is happening is that the Being of you is touched by the truth of what I'm saying. Other parts of you may also be triggered—your cynical part that protects you from disappointment in case I'm not really here, or your skeptical, more rational part that wants proof for everything.

Tanha: How do you want to be supported?

I have this deep feeling sense of things and I need support in expressing it. No one has ever believed in me before now and so I'm really gun-shy from being shot down. I need support from the part of you that could be strong for me in the world, an inner male who really knows my value and helps me put all my deep, formless sense of things into form and expression for me. There were times I felt so hopeless about ever being able to get my deep sense of Knowingness out of you, Tanha, and into some form of expression.

Tanha: What happened when you were inside me with no support?

I lived inside you in darkness for so long that I weighed you down and made you tired because there was no inner male to support and to help me out. I was being suppressed— without you even knowing it—by this other part that had no faith or belief in me whatsoever. This other part believed that everything about me was a lot of hooey unless I looked and acted and felt like a lot of other people do. It wanted conformity, and I was too different. I never got any messages that it would be okay to be myself, so I have been held down all this time until now.

I can't possibly begin to tell you how good it feels to be getting out. I am convinced that when I or any other parts are held down inside of people, they become depressed. And the bigger I am inside them, the bigger is their depression. If I can't be expressed physically or emotionally or sexually or spiritually or mentally, then I get clogged up inside them. Can you see what I mean?

Tanha: Yes I can. Tell me how you have dealt with this suppression.

I am such a survivor that I have found my ways to come out and get proper attention. For instance, who do you think it is who erupts into violent anger when I repeatedly am denied what I truly want? Or who do you think it is who breaks down into tears after long times of having my needs ignored? And who do you think it is who comes out if you get drunk? I am the part you have forbidden and hidden and been afraid of or ashamed of for so long. Who do you think causes disease? I am the part of you who is sick from lack of acknowledgment and attention. I am the four seasons, the four elements. If you deny me I come forth with great fury.

I am not evil. I am water that has been dammed and plugged. I burst forth with a vengeance and a distortion when I haven't been allowed my natural flow. I can burst forth with love or anger, generosity or selfishness, power or vulnerability, joy or grief, detachment or attachment, violence or gentleness—whatever has not been allowed expression.

If you deny me, I blaze forth in an uncontrollable erup- tion. If you say my sensual, sexual energy must be denied, I burst forth in an opposite kind of reaction. How much you push me down is how much I pop out in a way that distorts my beautiful, natural impulses.

Oh, I will not be stopped. I am life that must have its expression. I am bursting forth in nightmares and car acci- dents and even in depression and fatigue. I am like a rope

35

that keeps growing, and if there's no outlet for me to express myself, I start wrapping back around myself until I choke off my own life. When people ignore my needs and are too restricted to express me in many natural ways, I become uncomfortable in their bodies. So they drink and overeat and overindulge because they have nowhere that feels safe or acceptable to put me or use me. They hide me under the substances.

Tanha: Tell me more about this—about your feelings.

Don't you see who I am yet? I am your essential, instinctual response to each situation that life brings you. If I can't cry when I feel sad and I can't be mad when I feel mad, if I can't dream my daydreams and know my own desires, if I can't move toward people when I like them, and away from them when I don't like them, where can I go and what can I do? If I can't study what interests me, and believe what I believe and have the opinions and feelings that I have, what is left of me? That's when I become a robot. I am a robot that has been programmed so well it doesn't even know it's a robot and it runs around doing all the "right" things and feeling like something is missing. And if it doesn't realize it's acting out programs, then it's doomed to being a good robot all its life doing

> just what its parents want and
> just what its church wants and
> just what its community wants and
> just what everyone wants and it's called a pillar of
>   society and
> it dies of cancer and heart attacks.

I am here and you must have the courage it takes to own me. If you do—and if you learn to own me and cherish me and promise to trust and obey me in sickness and in health and in darkness and in light until death do us part—I promise that all the emptiness you have felt will become your fullness. I will guide you to what we most need to become whole, satisfied, fulfilled, giving, and contributing members of this world.

It won't be easy at first because you will have to learn to trust me more than anyone outside of you. You'll have to be willing to let go of the people in your life who won't like the real you that begins to emerge. But I promise you that people who are attracted to the real you will be your true friends—friends who want the same realness you long for, and they'll be willing to support your truth even if it hurts them at times. To me that's what real friends are, people who want to know the real you, not just people who want you to protect them from hurt and disappointment.

Tanha: What does it take to build a relationship with you?

It takes courage to believe in me and trust me after so many years of ignoring me. It takes time for us to build a relationship. It takes being conscious of the feeling of pain and loss of energy that comes from going against me—especially when it's just to keep the love of someone on the outside. It takes learning to communicate with people and letting them know how scary it feels to say no to them for fear they'll cut you off from their hearts. It takes a willingness to tell the truth about it when you don't listen to me, like that time Sarah asked you to drive all the kids to gymnastics. You said okay, but I was screaming inside, No No No! You were afraid to say no to Sarah because you wanted her to like you so much. When you finally told yourself the truth about what happened, it helped you and me. You felt that sick feeling of betrayal and loss for not honoring or at least communicating my feelings to Sarah, and trying to work something out with her. And remembering that sick feeling of betrayal has helped you not to get us in the same spot again. It has helped you speak up for what I want. I really think that's why people become dead-dissatisfied-lonely-lost-depressed-angry-sick: from always burying my needs and wishes and always saying yes when I am feeling No! Then their bodies feel really uncomfortable because my energy of no isn't allowed to move through them and be expressed. It gets stuck in the body, and that makes people want to do anything at all to get away from the discomfort. That's what causes physical addictions—trying to rid the body of uncomfortable feelings.

I want, I need, I lack.
I'm in your heart and I need you to hear me and feel me and see me and be with me.

I am real.
You can feel me in your body.
I feel feelings.
I need.
I want.
I desire.
I dream.
I have visions.

I can see what is possible.
Start acknowledging me, because the sickness of your
    planet comes from not believing that I count,
from not taking me into your counsel—not knowing what
    I have to offer.

There is only one way you could have gotten into this
mess and that is by denying my absolute importance to you.
I'd like you to learn to listen to me and to be my new parent,
the kind of parent we never had and always longed for.

Tanha: What kind of parent do you want me to be to you?

I'd like you to be a gardener-parent who comes out and
looks at me and appreciates me for who I am. If I have bugs
eating my leaves, remove them; if I need fertilizer, feed me;
if I need more light or more shade, give those things to me.
I'd like a gardener-parent who would let me grow to be
different than they are, who would see my uniqueness and
encourage it, curious to see what kind of flower I would
bear. I'd like a parent who derived great pleasure from
watching me grow and just being with me from time to time.
I'd like a parent to really look at me and see my special
needs and take time to listen and intuit and sense what they
are instead of assuming they always know. I'd like a parent
to steer me in the direction of my natural leanings so that
I am supported in whatever way is necessary to express my
particular gift to the world. I'd like a parent who under-
stands that I have the innate wisdom to grow into what I was
meant to be without their influence in that way. That's what
I'd like from you, my new parent.

dialogue between tanha
and the opposite parts

after hearing so much from my child's point of view I started to sense an uncomfortableness and pressure inside. I asked what this was all about, and discovered that other parts of me wanted to express their point of view.

Tanha: "Who are *you?*"

I am the protective, logical, rational, responsible part of you who also wants to be heard. I think this book you're writing is way too biased toward the side of the child. I'm afraid it will give readers the wrong impression about the way it really is and the way things work best for us. With all this stuff from the child, I can see people beginning to believe they should only listen to their child and forget about all the other voices inside them. So I want it to be stated, for the record, that I am hereby warning readers not to get too swayed by this one energy of the kid. She has some wonderful things to offer, no doubt, but each person has many valuable voices. The voices inside of you that are not the inner child also need to be heard and acknowledged. I can see

that Tanha's tendency to become addicted to this child's voice may lead others astray in the same way, and I don't think that is the wisest thing for them.

Tanha: Please go on. I'd like to hear from any other parts that need to speak.

Our job is to keep you in line so people will approve of you, respect you, and like you. We don't care if your creative expressions are stifled or your deepest dreams, desires, and longings never are expressed. Our job is to encourage people in the outside world to say, "This person is normal and together and acceptable because she looks like people should look and acts like people should act and dresses like people should dress."

We are here to make certain the person we live in will make no waves, for if they do they may be harshly judged and lose respect, validity, and credibility. We want each individual to have the support of the outer world because without it they might die, and our job is to ensure their survival. So we keep this child person hidden and in line.

We do a good job. We live inside of everyone and almost everyone allows us to run their lives. We don't support uniqueness, we support conformity. We're used to doing what will make others happy and what others expect us to do. We follow the written and unwritten rules of the society, the church, and the family. We are not accustomed to supporting the inner child.

We were invented for a good reason. We're the voices that say, "Go to college, invest in securities, get insurance, study something that will bring good money or prestige in our social circle, work at a regular job and stay with it whether you like it or not." We also say: "Don't make changes, be safe, don't tell the truth, stay comfortable, don't risk judgment from others, don't risk making a mistake, don't risk losing. In fact, don't risk at all." We are a status-quo bunch, and we're here to help this person survive in the family and culture they were born into.

Tanha: Do you think there's a problem with you running people's lives?

We know some change is needed because our way of operating hasn't been the greatest for the well-being of the individual or for the well-being of the world. In fact, we are considering a new order that would be of service to the inner child by helping her express herself and get what she wants and bring her visions into the world of form. We are beginning to trust that this inner child may be worthy of our respect, may even be worthy of our committed service and support, may even be a doorway for us to experience a feeling of purpose. We're beginning to suspect that with this kind of inner direction, our true purpose and fulfillment in life could be met.

The truth is, we're tired of running the show, but we're not certain how much of our previous function we still need to maintain. We are experimenting a little at a time, trying to listen to this Soul-Woman-Child and support some of the things she wants. We thereby risk outside disapproval, but we'll see how it works for us, and what happens. We're not willing to throw out the old order entirely, but we recognize that under our leadership people haven't been truly satisfied. There have been great technological accomplishments with us in charge, but the earth is very wounded and few people are finding deep contentment. We don't have the juice or the passion, the sensitivity or compassion, that she has. We do know how to get a job done, however.

We are getting ready to rest and play more of a support role. We are preparing to give the inner child a chance to direct and lead the show once again.

Tanha: It seems that you're a bit confused about your changing role with the inner child.

Yes, we are confused because our main job is to protect the inner child from judgment and shame, and yet we also see that she needs to be supported in expressing herself. We have helped her to survive by hiding her and that's what used to work for her. But what we hear now is that we need to support her in expressing herself instead of hiding her.

In fact, it was once a matter of life and death for us to protect her by hiding her. Now, she seems to be letting us know that it's a matter of life and death that she be able to come out of hiding and have us help her express herself. How can we protect her from being judged and shamed like before, if we help her do this? That is why we're confused about our role.

Tanha: You say you're concerned with the child's survival and pleasing people. I wonder why you have such strong protective feelings for the inner child.

Somehow, that beautiful and totally vulnerable inner child got the message from the world when she was younger that she was essentially worthless and valueless as she was and that she needed to be more like us to get any love, respect, or attention. We don't want to expose her to that awful feeling of being essentially bad ever again, so we would like her to be what everyone else wants her to be, just as we did when she was growing up. We just can't leave that beautiful and vulnerable child exposed to the possibility of feeling that awful feeling of being unacceptable as she is. Our job is to keep the love coming toward her so she never feels that deep shame again. We're extremely valuable in protecting the child from feeling worthless, as if she doesn't deserve to exist. That's an important part of our job.

We know that without us, you inner children wouldn't have survived, so don't judge us for being a "false self" or try to get rid of us. Give us some understanding and credit for what we've done for your inner child all these years, and understand that our job is to keep protecting her. Tanha, *you'll* have to be the one to sort this all out and decide whether to use us or not. Otherwise, we may keep on doing what we do.

Tanha: What if I decide not to use you as much as I have in the past? Will you still be there if I need you?

Yes, we'll always be here. In fact, you can be sure of one thing: if things get too stressful in a person's life, we become frightened and will always jump in to control. We can't help it. When the stress gets high enough, we are like smoke alarms—we go on automatically. We take over mostly under the stress of fear of failure, fear of judgment, and fear of survival.

part 3:

my story

my story

In this section, I want to share my process of getting to know my child. It's been one of the most important events of my life because now that we are connected again, I hardly ever feel the terrible pain I used to feel so often. And when we do get disconnected, I recognize her signals to me in my body and can easily find my way back to her. I've always cared about easing people's suffering. I hope that getting to know your child will help ease yours.

MY SEARCH FOR MYSELF

In 1974 I moved to California with the intention of finding myself. Looking back, I can see that I really needed to do this because I was what John Bradshaw calls the "lost child" in the family. When I remember my school years, I have only three memories of the first six years of school. Where did the rest of my memories go?

I was raised in a family who dictated to us children (there were seven) how we were supposed to think and feel. My family's religion also dictated how we were supposed to think and feel about a lot of things. Often my unique thoughts and feelings were not what they were supposed to be, and I was called a sinner and made to feel shame by the church and by my parents.

When I finished college and left home, I reacted to it all by throwing out most of the values, traditions, and ways of living that I had learned from my mom and dad, the church, and the civilized world. I didn't trust or believe in their ways, and I had never received any education that helped me to discover myself or what my own values might be.

It was a very painful time in my life. I was rebelling against all that I knew, and at the same time a critical voice inside my head was judging me severely for doing it. Because I had no values and beliefs of my own to use, I couldn't stand up to this voice; there was no inner support. I lived with a terrible not-knowing and emptiness that I didn't know how to deal with. It felt as if I had no solid ground to stand on and no tools for knowing how to find solid ground. I was extremely addictive then: to lovers, to alcohol, to the people who might give me some sense of myself, to the group that might have the answers. I didn't have *me*. I had thrown out God as I'd been taught to believe in Him and I was attempting to free myself of all my conditioning.

To find relief from the pain, I joined a cult of sorts, hoping to find a sense of safety and belonging. There, I believed I would once again establish a belief system and a set of values. For two years I tried to adopt the values and beliefs of that group, but it didn't work for me. The structure I needed was there, but the values and beliefs never felt true to my own inner wisdom.

After leaving this cult, I soon found another to join. The beliefs and values of this new group were more closely aligned with who I am, but as things began to radically change with them, I had the good sense to get out. Each time I left a group to follow my own inner feelings, instead of what they wanted me to feel, I was terrified because I didn't have faith in myself.

Now I can see that in all those years of searching I was try-ing to find out whether I could exist on my own without my family's and church's and culture's and cult's values and beliefs. My fear was always that I would fail to exist if I didn't belong to a group. My fear was that I wouldn't have the right to exist as I am; and if I dared to be me, I would once again be made to feel rotten to the core. And, as I first began to express myself, I did get that kind of judgment from my parents, but then I internal-ized my church's and parents' harsh judgment of my character, and had my own inner, self-critical voice to deal with.

In all my searching I desperately wanted to know my own boundaries—where I begin and others end. Since each of us is unique, and we perceive and value and believe things differ-ently, I wanted to know that none of us is fundamentally rotten to the core, that we are just different. I needed to know that I am a unique being with the right to explore that uniqueness and see where it takes me. To me that is the truest and most gratifying form of education—to set out on a journey of self-discovery.

MY LIFE IN MY ROOM

For the past ten years I have always worked in my home. In between clients I had a lot of time on my hands to live my life in my own rhythm. I was content to sit or lie on my couch for hours in a kind of trance state, pondering the mysteries of the universe and dreaming and fantasizing about things I wanted to do, but never following through with them. All that I thought and all that I understood and all that I experienced in this deep inner dream state was richly felt in some kinds of autumn vel-vety colors that had no form and just swirled around inside me.

Creative urges were building up inside me with nowhere to go. I wanted to write a book. I wanted to create transformational theater and write songs and sing them. These fantasies were designed to give me the pure joy of expressing myself, discovering my value, and helping others to realize that they were of value, also. But because I had learned that my thoughts and feelings, desires and visions, dreams and inspirations were of no value unless they matched those of my family and church, I felt it was impossible to believe in them or in myself.

There were times when songs were just bursting out of me. I'd sing them into a tape recorder because I couldn't bear to waste them, but it was too painful to listen to the tapes or to share them with anyone else. I believed that only other people's songs were good enough to listen to. I felt that way about my thoughts, too. Somehow I would value other people's thoughts and beliefs and opinions, if I was in harmony with them; but I couldn't give the same value to my own.

Those messages I had received from my family, church, and culture had coalesced into a critical voice in my head. This voice made me feel that I was of no value unless I was behaving and acting according to its beliefs and values. No wonder I was so lost somewhere deep inside. It wasn't safe to come out and be me.

I know that my parents were very concerned with doing the right thing for all seven of us, and they worked hard to do it. And, "God" was on their side. They were raising us the way they had been raised. In no way do I mean to blame them, but only to say my truth—which I hope will help expose the ignorance of parents in their treatment of their children.

Raising my own daughter has allowed me to feel compassion for my parents, and for all parents. There were things I did that were destructive to my daughter's self-esteem and I am sorry that I didn't know then what I know now. I don't want to blame myself either. I was doing my best and I was innocently unaware of any other way to raise her.

After many adult years had passed, a part of me started to push. It was a pressure from the inside, as if I would burst or die of depression and boredom if I didn't find some outlet for all the creative urges inside me. It almost felt like the urge to give forth my self-expression would push right through my skin.

I remember feeling that I couldn't go to one more workshop or read one more book about the human psyche. I had to open the faucet in me and let the flow go outward or I'd explode. Then a friend who has an abundance of that pushy energy I was feeling, started to encourage me to write a book. I told him that I felt overwhelmed because there was a world of things inside me that would like to be expressed, but that I had no idea how to begin to get them out. He gave me some very good advice that got me started. He told me to make an outline of what I'd like to include in a book. Being a person with so little structure in my life, I found this advice was enough to give me a skeleton to hang my ideas and creative thoughts on. Simultaneously, my inner child was telling me through our journaling exercise that she wanted to write a book. Then she wrote the outline for her section, and so I began.

GETTING TO KNOW HER

I had already become familiar with a part of me called the inner child. There has been a lot of talk about the inner child recently in the field of psychology. I knew that the rest of my personality was created to protect my child and that she has been in hiding because she hasn't felt safe or accepted in our world. People everywhere are now discovering the value of reconnecting with their inner child.

I met my inner child during a guided visualization exercise, as I mentioned in the introduction. In the exercise, you close your eyes and relax, while someone guides you on a journey into your imagination. One way to meet your child is to imagine that you see a child in the distance. As you come closer, you notice what the child is doing. As you approach it, you make contact in a way that feels natural to you. Maybe sit down beside it, or be quiet and wait until it's time to talk, or whatever seems right. Then you can ask your child what it needs from you and whether there is anything you can do for it.

Begin by having a dialogue with the child, which helps you to develop a sense of what it may be feeling or needing from you. Ask it questions and get to know it a little, so that you can start to build a relationship of trust. Let the child know whether you can give it what it has asked of you. If not, let it know what you *can* give. Because you're building a relationship of trust, it's important not to make promises you can't keep. You can also ask the child what it has to offer you. After you're together for a few minutes, or as long as you like, say good-bye and let the child know if you will be back to visit, and when.

My child was about four years old, and she was sitting beside a creek all alone. She was very somber, very contained, and very uncommunicative. I went to my inner child and asked what she needed from me. She looked at me as if to say, "I'm fine. Maybe it's you who needs something from me." I remember feeling rather put off by her. She seemed insulted that I had approached her as if I were a missionary coming to save her. She didn't look like she needed saving, and if she needed anything from me, it was for me to realize that fact. Her response surprised me and made me think.

I had one other encounter with my inner child in a visualization the following year. After those two experiences I began to accept the idea that there really is still a child inside each of us.

PSYCHOLOGY OF THE SELVES

When my therapist at that time asked to speak to my inner child, she used a method called voice dialogue. Doctors Hal and Sidra Stone devised this model based on the psychology of selves (*Embracing Our Selves*; see bibliography). The psychology of selves is the theory that the personality is made up of many selves or subpersonalities. Voice dialogue is a method that provides direct access to the different selves within us. Rather than spending sessions talking about certain thoughts, feelings, and behaviors, the facilitator can go directly to the self who has those thoughts, feelings, and behaviors and interview it. In this interview, the facilitator asks about what makes this part anxious, what its value and function is, what would have happened without it, and so on. This helps the voice to separate from the others and find the overseeing ego, which the Stones call the aware ego.

This process of voice dialogue provides the individual with access to inner information about the parts that make up the personality and also identifies a wiser decision-maker, which is the aware ego. The main goal of voice dialogue is to give birth to and strengthen our aware ego, the part of us that is not a voice, but that can make choices about whether or not to listen to and follow what the voices want. This part can begin to act as a wiser "parent" to the parts of us that have always run our lives.

When this aware ego is separate enough from the voices who have unconsciously run our lives, it then becomes safe for the more deeply hidden opposite parts to appear (for each voice has its opposite). For instance, a really hard-working person, always striving to achieve, has an opposite part that loves to do nothing and could care less about goals.

The way I see it, each of us has two sides: one is the masculine and one is the feminine. Within each side there are many, many voices or parts of us, each with its opposite. The masculine side has the more focused, active, goal-oriented, go-for-it, protective, survival-oriented parts. On the feminine side are the more open, diffuse, receptive, allowing, surrendered, wise, emotional parts, closer to the doorway to the Divine. In working with my voices and those of others in the past eight years, this is what I've learned. Of course, all the voices can't be categorized as strictly masculine or feminine—this is only a generalization of a pattern I have seen.

Often we become overidentified with one side or the other. And that's why the goal of voice dialogue—strengthening your aware ego—is so important. An aware ego allows us to become dis-identified with either side, so we are free to use the wonderful offerings of both.

For me, the inner child is on my feminine side. When I first discovered her, the development of the aware ego was the furthest thing from my mind. I was so relieved to find this energy of the child within me and so glad to find a way that allowed her total expression. It wasn't until years later that I started to realize the profound wisdom of the development of the aware ego. Until then I was caught up in the commitment of giving my inner child what she needed. I was seduced by her. I felt so good when she was here, as if my life had been waiting for her like a thirsty plant waits for water and attention. She seemed so wise. I devoted myself entirely to her needs and did what most of us do with one or two parts of us. I let her become number one in my life, and I judged, devalued, and refused to hear the information that was coming to me from the opposite selves. I suffered the results of the imbalance that it created: I started to believe that the inner child was me, and my closest relationships began to suffer.

After reading the Stones' second book, *Embracing Each Other* (see bibliography), I began to understand how my imbalance was responsible for causing problems in my closest relationships. It helped me to see what opposite energies or voices I needed to own in order to heal the imbalance that was creating the problems. Understanding this concept from *Embracing Each Other* has been the biggest help I have found in bringing clarity and joy in place of the pain and lack of life and passion in my close relationships. It helped me see what *I* could do to shift the relationship, rather than trying to get my partner to change.

BUILDING OUR RELATIONSHIP

When my inner child was reached during a voice dialogue session, I was able to become familiar with her because I could feel how she felt in my body when she was answering the facilitator's questions. I could experience the incredibly grounding, in-the-moment quality of her presence. It was then that I started to become fascinated with inner child work, because her presence brought such a delicious quality of energy to me.

I wanted to get to know her and to be able to consciously use her energy in my daily life.

I remember my inner child's attitude from the first visualization: "I have something for you; you don't have something for me." I began to realize that she held the qualities that were missing in my life. I had spent so much time thinking about the past and the future that I really hadn't felt the extreme pleasure of being present in my body with whatever experiences were here. The inner child carries the more essential wisdom, the "be here now" energy, so when I locked her away to act more like an adult, to find acceptance in the world, and to have some sense of control, I also locked away a lot of delicious things.

As I started to spend more time with her, I discovered that she's always delivering messages to me, and the only way for me to receive them is through the emotions and sensations I perceive in my body. By focusing on those sensations, I started to hear her messages to me. For instance, if I told someone that I was willing to be responsible for something when I really didn't want to be, my stomach would tighten. As I noticed the tightness and lightly held it within my focus of attention I could sense her saying, "I hate it when you always have to be such a perfect mother to Ami. You go right past my feelings and don't even take the time to hear me or consider my needs."

The good thing about being able to sense her messages is that after I really feel the discomfort and hear her communication, the discomfort clears. It is like a bundle of stuck energy that shows up somewhere in the torso to let me know something isn't okay, and as soon as I get the message, it passes through me. Sometimes a message doesn't come through, but just attending to the discomfort in that very gentle way allows the stuck energy to move on.

What I've learned is that it's our birthright to feel really good and clear inside, and when we don't, it's a good indication that something needs to be addressed. After it is, we'll feel good and clear again. It doesn't mean we always have to give our inner child what she wants—it just means we need to acknowledge what's happening.

One time, as I was beginning to value my inner child's input, I was trying to decide whether to travel to Denver, Colorado to lead workshops on my own. I was sitting in the backyard of my house and I decided to ask her what she felt about this. After I asked, I got such a heavy-duty response from somewhere inside that I started crying and crying. I heard or sensed her message to me:

> You have always pushed me to do all the things I was afraid to do, and now here's another thing that you want to push me to do and I don't like it. Traveling to some other city and staying alone in a hotel and being out there in the world like that with no one else is absolutely terrifying to me, and what I'd like is for you to stop doing big brave things like that until I say I'm ready to do them. If you listen to me and trust me, rather than push ahead and do important grown-up things, eventually you'll get just what you want. But first I want you to make me the most important part of your life and really learn to know me and build a solid relationship with me.

I remember feeling foolish as I responded to the strange voice I was sensing inside me. I was promising her that I wouldn't make her do all those big brave things and telling her that I would start proving how important she was to me by caring for what she wants. I was actually talking to this inner voice and vowing my devotion to her. Some other part of me thought this was a very strange thing I was doing. It was a life-changing experience for me.

For the next two years I didn't go out of town to work on my own. I started building my relationship with her. I put her first in my life and was willing to risk losing everyone that was dearest to me in order to prove to her that she came first. I was almost fanatical about it. If I felt any discomfort in my body after an interaction with someone, I would spend hours in my room trying to get a sense of what she was saying to me through that discomfort. If my partner and I had a date and she was having a problem, I'd break the date to be with her. I believed I needed to prove my commitment to her by giving her everything she wanted. Two years later, when things were really out of balance in my life, I realized that this was not a wise choice. I have more experience with inner voices now, and can see that they *all* want to run our lives. But like good parents, we don't want to let any of them take over; we just want to empower them all and listen to their thoughts and feelings.

WRITING WITH THE OPPOSITE HAND

I learned about a wonderful way of communicating with parts of myself from reading a book written by Lucia Capacchione (*The Power of Your Other Hand*, see bibliography); and I started communicating with my inner child by asking her questions with my dominant hand and letting her answer with my nondominant hand. Whenever I was feeling discomfort in my body from an interaction with someone on the phone or with one of my housemates, I would go into my room and ask the uncomfortable place in my body what the matter was. Then I'd let my left hand write the answer. This writing gives better access to the nondominant parts of the brain—the less conscious, the less familiar, the unknown. It helped my child to communicate to my conscious mind.

Through nondominant handwriting, my inner child let me know that she wanted to write a book, so I decided to ask her whether she happened to have an outline for the book she wanted to write.

I was sitting there very skeptically and anxiously, barely daring to hope that she really did have an outline, when she gave me three reasons why she wanted to write the book and five chapter headings. She said she'd like me to spend three hours with her every afternoon, letting her write. All I had to do was to provide the time and space, the nondominant writing hand, pen, and paper. She'd do the rest.

I was so thrilled to feel her response coming out from me in a way that felt so solid and real. Even though I had been in communication with her over a period of years, the skeptical side of me had always invalidated my experience of connection with her and doubted that it was real.

I was very excited to have such a clearly defined task ahead of me. We set out on the journey together, which involved my spending a lot of time with her for four months.

WHAT IT WAS LIKE BEING
WITH MY CHILD AS WE WROTE

Being with my child so intensely while she wrote this book was one of the most transformative experiences of my life.

Every day when I went to my room to let her write what she wanted, I was excited and curious to see what would come out. My respect for her grew. At the same time my respect for myself grew because I was willing to keep my commitment to her so completely, even in the presence of critical and skeptical parts of me that didn't want to give her any credence and didn't want me to proceed any further.

Some of those voices would have preferred that I had never responded to her desire or vision for this book, but had let her stay safe and hidden. They were positively frightened at the thought of showing anyone else what she had written. I had the sense that they felt they were fighting for our very survival when they were trying to stop me by saying things like, "Who do you think you are to think you know anything? How could anything of value come from you? How dare you think that you have anything to offer? How presumptuous, how full of pride you are to even value her enough to write down what she says." It was as if those parts wanted to kill me with criticism to save me from the judgment that would come from the world if I continued. But those parts seemed to change their opinion as we went along day after day. After several months of writing, they began to be amazed at what my inner child was writing.

WHAT HAPPENED INSIDE ME
DURING THE WRITING

There was something I found so nourishing about those months of working with my inner child. I'd look forward to every afternoon when we'd be together because it was so sooth-ing to be with her. As soon as I'd ask her a question and put my pen in my left hand to let her answer, I'd feel this delicious warm energy fill my body, which I started to recognize as her unique vibration.

As time went on, a change began to happen inside me. One afternoon, this change became clear as she was writing in response to a question I'd asked her. I had this strong sense that there was a very proper and scholarly Englishman looking over my shoulder, shaking his head and saying, "By jove, I believe she's got something here!" I felt his surprise and respect of her as well as his interest in what she was saying. And then in my imagination I saw and heard him call to some other fellows in his English club and invite them over to look at what she was writing.

After he showed himself to me, I realized that this man had been living inside me all these years. According to Hal and Sidra Stone, he represents the inner patriarch, the part of all of us that loves to conform with society's standards. He was the one who believed that everything I thought about that wasn't scientifically provable was just a lot of nonsense. He was the one who believed that intuition, coming out of nowhere and part of our inner wisdom, has absolutely no credence. He represented the entire western approach to living and education, which I consider a very left-brain, male-principle-oriented culture. And now he was expressing his interest in my inner wisdom and feeling that it had some validity. There was a huge shift in my consciousness that afternoon.

I have never felt the same since that experience. It felt as if there was an inner support I'd never had before. Something happened to my self-esteem as well. For most of my life I'd had a low self-esteem and all the affirmations in the world didn't seem to help. But after that experience, I started believing in my capability as a group leader and a teacher in a way I never had before. I started to follow through with more of my impulses. When I had an impulse that seemed to come from nowhere—like the impulse to invite a leader in my community out to lunch, tell her about my work, and ask her to help let people know about it—I followed through. A lot of work and income came to me from following this impulse. That proper English man was now supporting me, and for the first time I felt as if I had someone to believe in me, instead of being just doubtful, critical, and skeptical.

Another positive change occurred as I was writing the book with my inner child: my depression left. In its place I had tons of energy coming through me as I allowed myself and my inner voices to speak. This experience led me to believe that there is a powerful link between depression and a self or selves that are being held back.

HOW DIFFERENT ASPECTS
OF MY CHILD EMERGED

As I received my inner child's communication each afternoon, I became puzzled because she seemed to feel different to me than I expected a child would feel. At first, she seemed like someone who was screaming for me to connect with her and to start valuing what she was trying to say to me. As time went on and our relationship grew stronger, the part of my child that was so afraid, abandoned, and needy stopped appearing when I was writing with her. Over time, other, wiser, more spiritual parts of her began to emerge. I started to feel instructed by her, as if she knew things that all of us had forgotten and she was here to give us back the memory of our own wisdom and Knowing.

So I hesitate to call her my inner child; I also call her my Divine child, my feminine principle. She seems to express the personal part of me most closely connected to my spirit, like a point of balance between person and spirit. She keeps me feeling human when she talks about her feelings and needs; and at other times, she sounds and feels more related to spirit. She seems to have one foot in the world of the spiritual, but her emotional needs and curiosity keep her here on this earth plane. From her I get my visions and my deepest feeling values and desires. She seems to be the "creatress."

PROBLEMS WITH LISTENING SO INTENSELY TO JUST ONE VOICE

Because I was tuned in to my child and her needs to the exclusion of my opposite parts that are less personal and more detached, I was too open and unprotected. That meant I was sensitive to everything, so there was too much pain. The opposite voices serve to bring some sort of balance to the sensitive emotional availability of the inner child. They provide the distancing and cooler energy. Because the energy of my inner child was so permeable, diffuse, and receptive, I didn't have much of my action-oriented, male principle to work with. At times I was so open that I felt the collective sorrow of the world, and it was too much for me to bear.

Because I identified so completely with the feminine, open, soft, loving, and receptive energies, my daughter and my partner had to carry the more active, focused, impersonal, conservative, and task-oriented energies of the male side. That's what happens in our closest relationships. When one of us carries one aspect of our personality to such an extreme, those closest to us have to carry the opposite aspect. My outer relationships became very polarized and distant. As I learn to allow more of my male protective, impersonal energy into my work and relationships, my partner and my daughter experience more of the personal, warm energy that I had been keeping to myself. This brings us much closer since we are no longer so polarized. (This is another important principle that I learned from *Embracing Each Other*.) This understanding makes it easier for me to realize that I can't change the people I am in relationship with, but I can start to own the parts of me that I had pushed away—my action-oriented, male principle, more protective energies.

Becoming so identified with my child and all her sensitivity also made me want to isolate myself in my room because it felt like such a safe place. So instead of my world expanding, it became more and more limited. Thank God we naturally strive toward inner balance, because when I went to that extreme, the other parts of me started objecting so loudly that I had to hear them. My male side was saying, "Come on, we're bored, give us a challenge and a direction. Let's get on with life; let's get out into the world and give our contribution to it."

The male side of me is the aspect of my personality that helps me expand into the world. As long as he is willing to take direction from my wise, receptive feminine side, it feels really good to have him actively support us out there.

At that point I had a talk with my inner child and I let her know that I couldn't attend solely to her anymore. About the same time I had an appointment with a therapist. During the session I was extremely emotional, crying continually and talking about what my inner child needed. The therapist observed that all my concern was for my child, but none of it was for me. It was a shift in consciousness that gave "me" back to myself. There was me *and* my inner child, and it made me realize that taking care of the child isn't always a matter of saying yes to her. It's also saying "No, that's not what I want." It means having an awareness of myself as well. We both need to exist for this relationship to work. If I don't exist, I'm not available to hear from the opposite energies when they speak.

I had been warned by the facilitator who first helped me contact my child that I shouldn't put my entire attention on the child. But I've always been the type of person who has to find out for herself; and my child was so wonderful to be with, to the exclusion of the opposites.

What I now understand after eight years of working with my inner child is this: to get the most from my life I need to have one hand holding the vulnerable side, the other hand holding the impersonal, focused side. Another way to say this is that the feminine aspect (including the child) is on my left side, and the masculine aspect is on my right side. I stand in the middle of these unresolved conflicting selves. That is the ideal; however, I'm hardly ever able to do that. Instead, I become seduced by one of the sides and poof, I am that side, with no consciousness of the me that stands in the middle.

One of the things that helped me to dis-identify with my feminine energies was to engage my male side in the task of typing and editing this book. Producing rather than receiving brought a strength and protection back into my energy. Each day I realized how good it felt to have access to both my masculine and feminine sides.

GETTING THE MALE
AND THE FEMALE TOGETHER

I feel that I'm just beginning to know and appreciate the male voices inside me. A long time ago, I even tried to get rid of them and wanted to listen to the feminine side of me only. My mother had a very strong male side that she identified with and almost none of the feminine principle. Perhaps, in reaction, I developed a strong bias toward the feminine principle, which I still have. The western world also seems to be biased toward the male side, but I didn't relate to the lack of sensitivity and caring in it. It's not the job of the male side to care about things and people. It's not concerned with relatedness; it's just concerned with taking care of business.

As a sensitive child, I saw that male principle in action, especially in my mother. It felt dangerous to me, as if I would be run over by it, and I was. To avoid being that way, I adopted a strong female principle in a very imbalanced way. I have had to learn that the male principle is a good thing as long as it isn't used out of balance. I'm still learning to accept more of my male principle in order to balance my life and to heal my relationships with others. What I have discovered is that neither the male energies nor the feminine energies within us are good or bad. The problem is when we don't use both of them or when one side is running our lives without our knowing it. This can be destructive to ourselves and to others.

Shakti Gawain, a wonderful friend and teacher of mine, introduced me to the concept that our lives work best when our inner male supports our inner female. For me, if I get a feeling deep inside to do something that I have no logical reason to do, I'll follow up on that feeling by bringing in some support from the male side, which will make it possible for me to do what is wanted. I'm learning more and more to trust that deep, feminine, feeling sense that comes to me and to support it with my male side. It's like the love stories of old, only it's happening inside me. My gallant, honorable, and noble inner male is beginning to believe in the value and worth of my inner female, which is the source of all the feeling values, visions, and desires. He is ready for action, ready to honor her like the knights of old. He takes my deepest desires and helps bring them into the world of form. He made it possible to bring these thoughts and feelings from inside me to the outer world. He's my right-hand-man, and my Soul-Woman-Child is feeling more and more supported. The more support she feels, the more gifts flow from her.

In the past, it was very hard to do the things that seemed prompted by the male principle. In the late seventies and early eighties, when I was working as a masseuse, I would sometimes get to the point of having no money and become very anxious about it. The male protective parts of me would push me to buy a newspaper, look at the want ads, and get a job. Those promptings didn't come from my depths; they came from my fear, so it never felt like there was enough energy to carry me into action and follow up on that fear. For instance, I'd see an ad in the paper and make the call, but before I would hang up I would feel so devoid of energy that I knew I'd never make it to the interview.

That's why I believe we have to follow those deep promptings and urgings from our feminine side. They carry the energy that makes it possible for the male to follow through for her. They bring a feeling of wealth and satisfaction to us because we are doing what we truly feel like doing rather than doing what will ward off fear, or what someone else expects us to do.

In our western world, the masculine principle has pretty much been running the show and has been out of touch with the feminine and not in service to her. And when he's not in service to her, when the inner male principle doesn't have the direction of the inner feminine principle, things run amuck. Nothing seems to work right, and life becomes a struggle. The earth becomes pillaged. People go through their lives always headed somewhere in a hurry, hurrying to their deaths, without ever having the joy of being here.

What we're missing is the side of us that is always *here* and enjoying where we are, that is not necessarily always together and powerful, but is rather sensitive, shy, and vulnerable to what is happening in its environment. This is the part of us that's childlike and filled with awe when discovering a dew drop on the end of a blade of grass, the part of us that is truly present and available to people, to intimacy, to relationship with one another and the world, and the part of us that has a Knowing that comes from our deep inner well.

That is why my inner Soul-Woman-Child believes that many wrongs in the world can be righted by each of us learning to connect with our inner female's deepest desires, visions, and leanings, and by having our inner male support her by making her real in the world. If our inner male acts in support of the wisdom of our inner female, everything will be connected correctly. There will be right direction and right timing and right action.

MEDITATION

To bring balance between the inner male and female, the inner child and its opposites, and our other voices or parts, requires being able to separate from the parts. It requires an awareness of the "me" that is not just one part. At the beginning of my journey of self-discovery, I went to a two-week meditation retreat. For ten hours a day, we simply sat and observed our thoughts and felt the experience of our breath entering our bellies and then leaving our bellies. I discovered a vast spaciousness inside me that felt as if I had been home for the first time since I was born. When we had our break, I was so filled with joy that I couldn't contain it and went singing through the mountains, "I'm home, I'm home."

Probably the most important transformation of my life came from truly experiencing, rather than praying to, this Home that I really am one with. I found that there was so much more available to me than just the limited experience of my personality's selves or voices. For the first time, I knew God—I was connected with the Divine. After this initial retreat, I became very interested in meditation and was lead to a teacher.

For the past eight years, I have had an incredible guide to the Divine in my teacher, Don Kollmar. He trains people to guide others in this process as well. His two tapes, *Coming Home to Self I* and *Coming Home to Self II* (see bibliography) will assist people who have been longing for connection with their soul. His work is called the complete self-attunement method. It is a way to tune into the constant emergence of our Being. Because we're used to listening to nothing but the vibrations of our personal selves, or voices, this has caused confusion inside: we have thought the selves to be *us*. Don teaches us how to tune into the more subtle energy of our life force by almost listening, feeling, and sensing from each cell of the body, training ourselves to listen from what he calls the seventh sense, the body sense. By tuning into that more subtle and refined energy, we can start to feel our Essence emerging. The experience of our Essence is large enough to include all of our personality's selves. It allows us to give them the attention and love they are asking for.

This work has been a beautiful experience for me because it has allowed me to spend very healing and regenerative time with my Being and to reconnect with my true nature. Meditation has continued over the years to quench a deep thirst in me for spirit, and I highly recommend it to anyone who has the same longing.

I was raised in a very religious family in the Catholic religion, and went to Mass every day from the seventh grade through high school. For years, I longed for connection to God, and meditation has given me what no other church has been able to, the experience of God that I've longed for. It has taught me how to use my perception to tune in to the more subtle energy of my life force, and then from my heart center to ask for the Divine to emerge.

I have a strong suspicion that all of us are evolving into a consciousness that will allow both the Divine and the human to exist at the same time, without leaving either one out or judging one better or worse. That is certainly what I'm most deeply longing for. But maybe the nature of being human is to keep getting lost in a part of our personality, thereby losing touch with our true nature.

I guess grace or evolution will have to bring me my desire, because I can't make it happen on my own. Instead of trying to make it happen, what I say is, "I'm open to receive this experience of my wholeness in the very midst of my life, for the highest good of all." That's an interesting thing about our connection with the Divine. It has to be approached from the side of us that is willing to surrender because it's all about allowing —allowing all of our parts to exist and allowing our deep inner well to bring forth what's needed.

We can't reach our Divinity from the part of us that is determined to make it happen. All we can do is create the time and space and bring our attention to the sensing of our inner experience. We can notice that the trier is trying and the thinker is thinking, and then keep noticing and sensing whatever else is happening within our inner experience. All we can do is to provide the right environment into which the Divine can enter. The rest is up to the Divine.

inner child meditation

$$\mathbf{I}\text{nstructions:}$$

Have someone read this to you very slowly, or tape it for yourself. It's written from your inner child to you. If it doesn't suit you and your inner child, ask your own inner child to write one for you through your non-dominant hand.

Close your eyes and promise me your time and attention. Come into my world of the body with me and say goodbye to your world of the mind.

When you're feeling bad or sad or mad, I'm here in your body trying to get your attention.

Please don't abandon me now and start thinking about what's making you feel bad. That doesn't help me. You help me most by being with me in our body.

Take a deep breath and as you breathe out, fall a little deeper into our body. I live here. Come be with me where it feels uncomfortable in your torso.

I'm right in here. Don't hover too close to me and smother me. Just let your attention rest near me in that area. That helps me to know I'm not alone. It helps me to let go because I feel your love and I don't have to grab on so tight. It lets me tell you any words if I need to.

Now you're in here, resting near me. We can just be here, both of us together resting as the body breathes us up and down. Notice what it's like to just be here feeling the sensations of the body together. Just being together. (I'll let you know when we've had enough by how I feel.)

Thank you for being with me. Come back soon when I need you. Bye.

Commentary:

You'll see, the more you're willing to be with me like this when I need you, the more something bigger than us starts to emerge as I calm down. And pretty soon we're both resting in Larger Arms being totally loved and attended to.

It's magic and mystery. Some people call it

Essence
others The Void
others God
others our True Nature
others the Universe.

But no matter what you call it, the body, and my anxiety or tension or anger or grief held within it, are the doorways to *spirit*, and all you have ever longed for.

conclusion

In order to write this book, I had to keep letting go of my ideas of how it should be, and stay with what was unfolding organically. For instance, I thought my very vulnerable, wounded child was going to be the author. On the days we were writing together, she was always there in the beginning, afraid that nothing would come out of her that had value. Once I attended to her feelings, she seemed to feel loved. Then it seemed like she opened up into a wise, knowing being that had a lot she wanted to say. Is that what happens when we give the vulnerable child the attention she needs? I wondered. She blossoms right in front of our eyes into the wise knowing one?

For the almost two years of transforming the early writing into this book, the wounded child wasn't around very much. I thought that meant that she had transformed into the wise one because I had given her so much love, respect, and attention.

But two months ago, something happened in my life that brought her up again full force. I asked her yesterday why she disappeared when we were writing the book and she answered through my nondominant hand:

I hurt. I live in you. I'm not enough. Something is wrong with me. I'm really not okay. You keep me hidden. I need

love and acceptance from everyone we meet and you want to hide that from people. In your family I wasn't acceptable. I want to write a book with you too. I want everyone to know that I live in them and that I'm loveable even when I'm just raw need.

I like it when you let your therapist see me and see my need. I like it that she's not afraid of me. When you show me to her like I have asked, I feel like you love me then. I wish you could show me to everyone in the world. That would feel really good to me. Then I wouldn't be so ashamed of being here. I want them to accept me. I want you to accept me, too. I count too even though I need so much love.

This process of journeying with my child still has many unanswered questions. I still feel that I'm just beginning to learn how to be with the very wounded one and give her what she needs.

Before I wrote this book and had the experience of tuning in so directly and closely with my child sides and then my protector sides, I thought that if I totally devoted myself to my child that would be the best purpose I could have for my life, because she felt so closely connected to what's real in me, to my essence. From being with her so fully, and then from having my more protective side come out unexpectedly, I have developed a deep sense of value for both sides. Before, I had wanted to discount my male protector side because it didn't feel real, or authentic, or as much me as the child. It felt like my parents, or like society. Now I see more clearly that it really wants to protect me. It can hold within its memory all the things that didn't go right in the past, and remind me about them for any decision I want to make now. My child side just sees what she wants and somehow believes that what was painful to her before won't be painful now. That's why so many people end up repeating painful relationships. They are listening to only one side of themselves instead of staying current with both sides.

Now I have an incredible respect for both sides of me. I see the value they each have. I'm willing to feel the uncomfortable ambivalence within me when they are each allowed to live and each can give me their point of view and opinion.

My wish for you is that this book will help you identify the side of you that is running your life and develop a value and a respect for it. I also wish you will be able to allow the other side of you to exist in its full value and beauty. I hope you will trust that somehow in holding the awareness of both in the moment, your true nature will proceed forward into your life with its purpose here fully expressed.

I first committed so fully to my child because I was on a search for my Essence or my true nature. I have discovered from meditation that my Essence is far beyond and much greater than any of the voices. In my new understanding, I see that although my child is not my Essence, attending to her feelings is a doorway to my Essence or to the Divine.

Those of you who have read this book must be very interested in connecting with your own inner child, so I wanted to share that Lucia Capacchione has a recent book out called *Recovering Your Inner Child*. Her other books have been so helpful to me in connecting with my child, I'm sure this one will be too.

Thank you for sharing my journey with me. I hope it will be helpful to you.

With love,
Tanha

bibliography

Capacchione, Lucia. *The Power of Your Other Hand: A Course in Channeling the Inner Wisdom of the Right Brain.* North Hollywood, California: Newcastle Publishing Co., Inc., 1988.

Capacchione, Lucia. *Recovery of Your Inner Child.* New York, New York: Simon & Schuster/Fireside, 1991.

Gawain, Shakti. *Living in the Light.* San Rafael, California: New World Library, 1986.

Gendlin, Eugene, *Focusing.* New York, New York: Bantam Books, 1981.

Kollmar, Don. *Coming Home to Self I and II.* For information about the complete self-attunement process or workshops with Don Kollmar, write CSA Asociates, P.O. Box 1376, New York, New York, 10028 or call (212) 734-0930.

Levine, Stephen. *A Gradual Awakening.* Garden City, New York: Anchor Books Doubleday, 1979.

Levine, Stephen. *Meetings at the Edge.* Garden City, New York: Anchor Books Doubleday, 1979.

Levine, Stephen. *Who Dies.* Garden City, New York: Anchor Books Doubleday, 1982.

Steinbrecher, Edwin C. *The Inner Guide Meditation.* York Beach, Maine: Samuel Weiser, Inc., 1989.

Stone and Winkelman. *Embracing Each Other: Relationship as Teacher Healer and Guide.* San Rafael, California: New World Library, 1989.

Stone and Winkelman. *Embracing Our Selves.* San Rafael, California: New World Library, 1989.

OTHER BOOKS AND TAPES
FROM NATARAJ PUBLISHING

Books

Living in the Light: A Guide to Personal and Planetary Transformation. By Shakti Gawain with Laurel King. The recognized classic on developing intuition and using it as a guide in living your life. (Trade paperback $9.95)

Living in the Light Workbook. By Shakti Gawain. Following up her bestseller, *Living in the Light,* Shakti has created a workbook to help us apply these principles to our lives in very practical ways. (Trade paperback $12.95)

Return to the Garden: A Journey of Discovery. By Shakti Gawain. Shakti reveals her path to self-discovery and personal power and shows us how to return to our personal garden and live on earth in a natural and balanced way. (Trade paperback $9.95)

Awakening: A Daily Guide to Conscious Living. By Shakti Gawain. A daily meditation guide that focuses on maintaining your spiritual center not just when you are in solitude, but when you are in the world, and especially, in relationships. (Trade paperback $8.95)

Embracing Our Selves: The Voice Dialogue Manual. By Drs. Hal and Sidra Stone. The highly acclaimed, groundbreaking work that explains the psychology of the selves and the Voice Dialogue method. (Trade paperback $12.95)

Embracing Each Other: Relationship as Teacher, Healer, and Guide. By Drs. Hal and Sidra Stone. A compassionate guide to understanding and improving our relationships. The follow-up to the Stone's pioneering book on Voice Dialogue. (Trade paperback $11.95)

Maps to Ecstasy: Teachings of an Urban Shaman. By Gabrielle Roth with John Loudon. A modern shaman shows us how to reconnect to the vital energetic core of our being, by showing us how dance, song, theater, writing, meditation, and ritual can awaken the healer in each of us. (Trade paperback $9.95)

Notes from My Inner Child: I'm Always Here. By Tanha Luvaas. This deeply touching book puts us directly in contact with the tremendous energy and creativity of the inner child. (Trade paperback $8.95)

Coming Home: The Return to True Self. By Martia Nelson. A down-to-earth spiritual primer that explains how we can use the very flaws of our humanness to carry the vibrant energy of our true self and reach the potential that dwells in all of us. (Trade paperback $12.95)

Corporate Renaissance: Business as an Adventure in Human Development. By Rolf Osterberg. This groundbreaking book explodes the myth that a business's greatest asset is capital, and shows why employees must come first for businesses to succeed in the 90s. (Hardcover $18.95)

Tapes

Living in the Light: Shakti Gawain Reads Her Bestseller. (Two cassettes $15.95)

Developing Intuition. Shakti Gawain expands on the ideas about intuition she first discussed in *Living in the Light.* (One cassette $10.95)

To Place an Order

Call 1-800-949-1091.

Nataraj Publishing is committed to acting as a catalyst for change and transformation in the world by providing books and tapes on the leading edge in the fields of personal and social consciousness growth. "Nataraj" is a Sanskrit word referring to the creative, transformative power of the universe. For more information on our company, please contact us at:

Nataraj Publishing
P.O. Box 2627
Mill Valley, Ca. 94942
Phone: 415-381-1091
Fax: 415-381-1093